Contents

Time for fun

There are times when people have a rest from work, such as:
- playtime at school
- weekends
- holidays.

Times like these are called **leisure** time. They are times to have fun.

- What do you like to do to have fun in the school holidays?
- Where did you go for your holidays last year?
- Have you ever been on a ride like the Vortex? How did it make you feel?

WHERE YOU LIVE
Do a survey of people you know, to find out their favourite leisure activities.

You can have fun on your own and with other people.

There are many types of places where people go to have fun.

G FLAMES

Guildford Flames Ice Hockey Club

NEXT HOME MATCH VERSUS SHEFFIELD

DATE SATURDAY 30th DECEMBER

TIME 6.00pm

Outdoors and indoors

Many people like to spend some of their leisure time outdoors.

See how many activities you can think of that only take place outdoors.

Some activities need a particular type of weather.

Some activities need a special type of **landscape**: for example, hills for down-hill cycling. Others need special **facilities**, like a football pitch.

- What type of weather do you need to fly a kite?
- What leisure activities can people take part in when it snows?
- What leisure activities do people take part in where there is a river?

Think of buildings where people go to have fun, such as:

- **museums**
- **amusement arcades**
- bowling alleys
- **cinemas.**

WHERE YOU LIVE
Investigate the 'Having Fun' section at the front of your local telephone directory.

- What activities are there at the museum on the right?
- What is the name of your nearest cinema?
- How far do you have to travel to get to the cinema?

Sports and leisure centres

Many towns and cities have sports and leisure centres. Some leisure centres are built near to schools so that children can use them during the day.

Junior Activities

Complete the application form in the back of this booklet to enter your child on the waiting list, hand back into the Centre once completed. Please note some waiting lists are longer than others. The Course co-ordinator will contact you when a place becomes available.

Football

Both Boys & Girls are welcome to join in on the fun and improve skills at the same time.
Lots of opportunity to play matches and make new friends.

Wednesday:	5.15pm - 6.15pm	5yrs+
	5.30pm - 6.30pm	5yrs+
Friday:	6.30pm - 7.30pm	8yrs+ Improvers

Trampolining

Claire, Hannah and Sarah are all B.T.F. fully qualified coaches. Join them and they will help your child improve suppleness and trampolining techniques while having lots of fun!!!
Sessions are available for children aged 5yrs and above.

Monday:	6.30pm - 7.30pm
	5.30pm - 6.30pm
Thursday:	6.30pm - 7.30pm
	9.30am - 10.30am
Saturday:	10.30am - 11.30am
	11.30am - 12.30pm
	12.30pm - 1.30pm

Badminton

All abilities welcome to learn and improve their stroke, game techniques and racket skills.

Saturday:	11.30am - 12.30pm	8-16yrs

Gymnastics

Recreational Gymnastics for all abilities. These sessions are ideal for developing your children's co-ordination, flexibility and balance while learning new skills and having fun!!! All these sessions take place on a **Saturday** at the following times:

9.45am - 10:30am	3-4yrs
10.35am - 11:15am	5-6yrs
11:15am - 12:00pm	Mixed Ages
12:00pm - 1:00pm	6-7yrs Improvers
1:30pm - 2:30pm	7-8yrs Improvers
2:30pm - 3:50am	9yrs+

Dance

Book your children in and benefit from the use of our brand new dance studio. Ballet & Jazz dance classes are excellent for developing your childs balance, co-ordination, flexibility and gives them the opportunity to make new friends. Classes include:

Thursdays	4:30pm - 5.00pm
	5.00pm - 5.30pm
Saturdays	10.00am - 10.30am
	10.30am - 11.00
	11.00am - 11

Spaces ...le on

- How many activities are shown in the leisure centre's leaflet above?
- What game are the girls on the left playing?
- Why do leisure centres open in the evening as well as in the daytime?

Some leisure centres are owned by the local **council**. The council uses some of the **tax** that people pay to run the centre.

At a leisure centre you can join classes to learn sports such as swimming, karate and trampolining.

In some bigger towns and cities there are ice **rinks** (right) or indoor snow centres, where you can ski or snowboard.

•What activity would you like to learn at a leisure centre?
•What jobs do people do at a sports and leisure centre?

WHERE YOU LIVE
Do a class survey to find out where people go to take part in sports.

What's on?

Most towns and cities have one or more cinemas. Some have **theatres** or concert halls, too. Many new cinemas are built on the outskirts of town. Some are multiplexes with three, four, or more screens.

• What was the last film you saw at the cinema?
• What information must a poster give about a film or a play that is coming on?

You can look in a local newspaper to find which films, plays and concerts are coming. See if the paper has a section called 'What's on'.

Posters and **banners** also tell you what films and shows are coming to town.

WHERE YOU LIVE
Look for posters that advertise local events and entertainments. Are some events for children?

Film shows, plays and concerts also take place in **village halls**, churches, schools and in the open air. Pantomimes are often performed in the winter.

In a theatre and at a cinema, the place where you buy your ticket is called the **box office** (right). You can also buy tickets on the phone or over the internet.

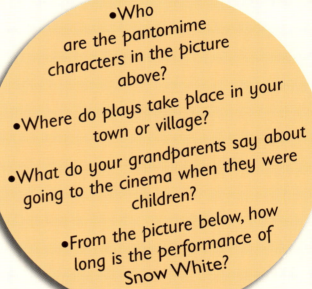

- Who are the pantomime characters in the picture above?

- Where do plays take place in your town or village?

- What do your grandparents say about going to the cinema when they were children?

- From the picture below, how long is the performance of Snow White?

THIS PERFORMANCE

Begins At   Ends At

SURREY ADVERTISER 50p

Theme parks and zoos

Theme **parks** are full of exciting rides, stalls and games. They are usually built away from towns and cities, where there is plenty of space.

- Which three words would you choose to describe the rides at a theme park?
- Where is your nearest theme park?
- Why are theme parks closed in the winter?

WHERE YOU LIVE
Think of all the things that go to make a good theme park. Draw a plan of what you think a good theme park should be like. Draw in all the paths and the places for the different rides.

- Which are your favourite animals at a zoo? Why do you like them?
- Which country does your favourite type of animal come from?
- Which is the nearest zoo to where you live?
- In the picture below, which way must you turn to go to the zoo? Where is 'The Serengeti'?

There are zoos in some of the large towns and cities in the UK. Some people don't like the idea of animals being kept in zoos, but some zoos have helped to **preserve** rare animals.

On road signs and maps, the symbol for zoos and wildlife centres is usually an elephant.

↑ Houghton Regis

← Kensworth

AA Lions Of The Serengeti ←

15

Eating out

People eat out at **cafés**, **pubs**, **restaurants** and hotels. At these places there is lots of work for **chefs**, cooks, kitchen **staff**, waiters and waitresses.

- What work must people do in the kitchen of a restaurant?
- What is good about working in a restaurant? What is bad?
- What is your favourite type of food? Which type do you least like?

Caffé Piccolo
Ristorante Italiano
01252-723277

CHINA EXPRESS
豐 恆
DELIVERY   CHINESE TAKE-AWAY   227633

Caffé Piccolo
Ristorante Italiano
01252-723277

Aladdin INDIAN TAKEAWAY
— FREE HOME DELIVERY SERVICE —
TEL:267667

- Which countries are represented in the restaurant signs in these pictures?
- What do you like to eat on a picnic?
- What symbol is used on a road sign for a picnic site?

In the past, most restaurants in the UK sold 'British' food, like roast beef and Yorkshire pudding, or fish and chips. Now, many towns have restaurants that serve food from all over the world.

A different way of 'eating out' is to have a picnic, or to get a 'take-away'.

WHERE YOU LIVE
Find cafés and restaurants that serve food cooked in the style of other countries.

17

Parks and play areas

A park is a piece of land in a town, where people can enjoy being outdoors. Many of the biggest parks in the UK were built in **Victorian** times.

- Which season does this picture show?
- What does a park look like on a street map?

Towns also have play areas for children who live in houses and flats nearby. Many play areas include a grassy field, swings and a climbing frame.

There are rules in play areas and parks. One rule may be: 'Cyclists must stay on the paths.'

Another rule may be: 'Do not pick the flowers.'

- Why would it be wrong to cycle on the grass?
- What other rules do you think there should be in a park?
- What do people like to look at in a park?
- What do people like to do in a park?

If people keep the rules, the park stays enjoyable for everyone.

WHERE YOU LIVE
Visit a park. Make a list of everything you can find that helps people to enjoy themselves in the park.

Clubs

Some people belong to clubs and organisations, such as a football club, an art club, Brownies, Guides, Cubs or Scouts.

1st Churt Scout Group
www.haslemeredistrictscouts.org.uk

These Brownies are singing a song together.

• What is the scout **motto**? (You can see it on the scout hut notice above.)

• Do you belong to a club? What is its name and what does the club do?

• What work do the leaders of a club do?

Some clubs and organisations have their own buildings.

Others meet in village halls or sports centres.

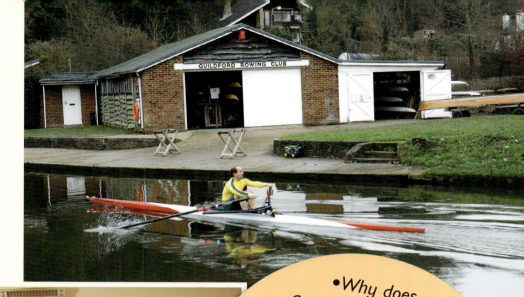

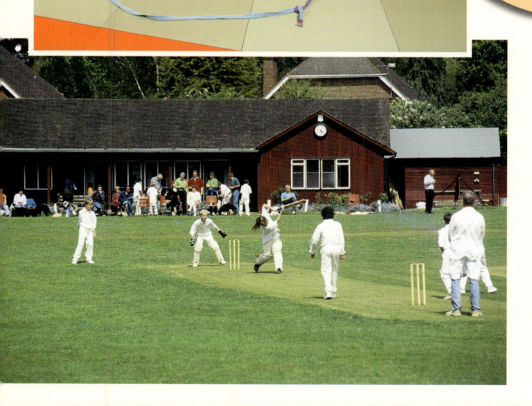

- Why does a rowing club need a building by the river or canal?
- What club do the children in the photograph (left) belong to?
- What do you think the cricket club members (below) use their **pavilion** for?
- Which sports team do you support? Where do you go to watch the team play?

Some sports clubs have their own sports ground and a building beside it called a pavilion. The pavilion is used by the players and by the people who go to watch and support them.

City sights

Many people like to visit big cities, like London, Birmingham, Cardiff or Edinburgh for a fun day out, or even a weekend break.

Big cities are full of amazing buildings to see, like the Tower of London (right) or Brighton Pavilion (below).

• Why do you think people like visiting places like the buildings on this page?

You can even tour some cities on an open-top bus, like this one.

City museums are interesting places to learn about history, science and natural history.

- What two things make up the symbol for a museum (top) that is used on road signs and maps?
- What types of objects have you seen in a museum?

Art galleries have exhibitions of paintings and sculptures from the past and the present.

You can find out all about places to visit in a town or city at a tourist information office (right).

- What does the 'i' stand for in the tourist information symbol?
- What are three types of information that people ask for at a tourist information centre?

Tourist Information

WHERE YOU LIVE
Design a poster that would attract visitors to your nearest big town or city.

Seaside holidays

The pictures on this page give information about holidays in the past. The top two photographs show people at the seaside in Wales in 1898.

- How many years ago were the top two photographs taken?
- What are the people doing?
- Which seaside places have the children in your class been to?
- How did they travel there?

In 1905 a young boy received this postcard from his aunt. She wrote, 'Dear Jackie, This is the Puff Puff that will take you to Bournemouth for your holidays.'

Be Quick Puff Puff I want to get to the Sea

BOURNEMOUTH EXPRESS, L. & S.W.R.

Seaside places have different types of beaches, such as sandy or pebbly. There may be tall **cliffs** at the back of the beach. There may be a **promenade** to walk along.

Some places have a **pier** sticking out into the sea. It may have cafés, shops and an amusement arcade or even a helter-skelter on it.

CRAZY GOLF

• Which three things do you think are important for a good seaside holiday?

• What differences are there between the photo of the children on the beach below and the photo on the opposite page?

WHERE YOU LIVE
Make a display of pictures that give information about seaside holidays today.

Local events

Travelling entertainers may come to your town or village and set up a **fair** or a show, such as a circus, for a while.

The picture above shows a circus **big top**, which was put up on an area of grass called the **common**.

- What happens at a circus?
- Which country does the circus in these pictures come from?
- Where do local outdoor events take place in your town or village?

One of the lorries was used as the box office for the circus.

Sometimes people who live in a place organise a **street party**, a **fête** or a local **carnival**. These events encourage local people to have fun together. Some of the events are held in order to raise money too.

- What type of things do people try to raise money for at a fête or carnival?
- Have you been in or watched a carnival parade? What was it like?
- Which time of year is best for a street party?

WHERE YOU LIVE
Plan a school fête. When would be a good time for it? What stalls and entertainments would there be?

Glossary

Amusement arcade A hall with many video games and machines for gambling.

Banners A strip of material that is hung across a street. It is called this because it is like the banner (a type of flag on two poles) that people sometimes carry in processions.

Big top A large circular tent used for a circus. The circus performers use the ring in the middle. Seats for the audience are arranged all round the ring.

Box office The office where tickets can be booked for a play, film or other show.

Café A place where food and drink are served to customers. At a café, the food is usually more simple and less expensive than at a restaurant.

Carnival A fun event where people dress up to be part of a procession through their town or village centre. There are also entertainments to watch and a fair.

Chef The head cook in a hotel or restaurant. Chef is a French word for 'head' or 'leader'.

Cinema A building where films are shown.

Cliffs High, steep rocks at the edge of a piece of land, where the land ends and the sea begins.

Common An open area of land that belongs to a town.

Council A group of people who run a town, a district or a county.

Facilities Things that are provided so that people can take part in activities if they wish.

Fair A type of market with amusements and rides as well as things for sale.

Fête An outdoor event with entertainments, stalls and refreshments.

Landscape What the countryside looks like.

Leisure Time away from work to do what you want.

Motto A short saying that organisations use, like a badge, to represent what they do. For example, 'Be prepared' is the motto of the Scouts.

Museum A place where objects are collected and put on display for people to study.

Pavilion A building by a sports ground. It includes facilities for the sports players, such as changing rooms and showers and places to relax after a game.

Pier A long structure that sticks out into the sea.

Poster A large, printed advertisement that is stuck up in places where lots of people will see it.

Preserve To save something from becoming extinct, or dying out.

Promenade A wide, paved walkway along the back of the beach in some seaside places.

Pub A short name for a 'public house'. Pubs are buildings where alcoholic drinks are the main thing that is served.

Restaurant A place where meals are prepared and served to the customers.

Rink An area of ground or floor made suitable for skating.

Staff All the people who work in a place.

Street party A party for everyone who lives in a street, often with tables arranged in the road. Sometimes street parties are held to celebrate an event like the queen's birthday.

Tax Money that all grown-ups pay so that it can be used to provide things that the whole community needs, such as schools, street lights and rubbish collection.

Theatre A place with a stage where drama is performed. Many theatres have seats arranged in rows, with higher rows at the back so that everyone can see the stage well.

Theme park A large park with many fairground rides. The words 'Land', 'Kingdom' or 'World' are often used in the names of theme parks and in the names of different areas inside a theme park. Everything in the park, or in the area, makes it look like a certain type of place.

Victorian During the reign of Queen Victoria, who was queen from 1837 to 1901.

Village hall A hall that was built to be used for local events and activities.

Further information

Where you live, you can find out about the entertainments that people take part in by looking at the local newspaper, notices and posters around your town or village, and the 'Having Fun' section of your local telephone directory. There is also information about clubs, activities and places to visit at your local library and at a tourist information office.

Useful websites

http://www.woodlands-junior.kent.sch.uk/customs/topics/index.htm
has useful information for projects about Britain. You can look up a topic, such as Leisure time and Sports, in the long A to Z list.

Find out about Beavers, Cubs and Scouts at http://www.scouts.org.uk/
There are links to sites for Rainbows and Brownies at http://www.girlguiding.org.uk/

The Bethnal Green Museum of Childhood in London has collections of toys and games. You can see some at http://www.vam.ac.uk/moc/index.html

At http://www.24hourmuseum.org.uk/ you can search for museums that tell you about a particular subject or museums in a particular part of the UK.

A map of places for school trips is at http://www.educationalvisitsuk.com/map.asp, with links to information about each place.

http://www.themeparks-uk.com/ has links to the websites of all the main theme parks in the UK.

You can find out more about seaside holidays at
http://home.freeuk.com/elloughton13/seaside.htm

'Footprints in the Sand' is a website with pictures and information about the history of two seaside towns, Torbay and Bournemouth:
http://www.swgfl.org.uk/seaside/

The website of the National Piers Society, http://www.piers.co.uk/, has some 'Pier Facts'. Also click on 'Piers' for pictures and information about every pier.

Books

Growing Up in World War Two: Entertainment, Catherine Burch, 2005 (Franklin Watts)

Life in the Past: Victorian Seaside Holidays, Mandy Ross, 2005 (Heinemann Library)

Ways Into History: Seaside Holidays, Sally Hewitt, 2004 (Franklin Watts)

Ways Into History: Toys and Games, Sally Hewitt, 2004 (Franklin Watts)

Why Manners Matter: Playing in the Park, Jillian Powell, 2005 (Franklin Watts)

A Walk in the Park/A Walk by the Seaside, Sally Hewitt, 2005 (Franklin Watts)

Index